MURPHY WAS A LAWYER ...
AND A QUAHOGGER

Selections from Murphy's Law
by John Austin Murphy
illustrated by Don Bousquet

For Beverly L.
— a true
Jamestowner !
Best wishes
John Austin Murphy
Dec 4, 2006

Published by Tashtassuc Press

Copyright© 2005 by John Austin Murphy

All rights reserved under International and Pan-American Copyright Conventions

Published in the United States by Tashtassuc Press, a division of Jay Associates
77 Narragansett Avenue, Jamestown, Rhode Island 02835-1149
Distributed by Tashtassuc Press
JohnA@Murphys-Law.net
Tashtassuc Press is a trademark of Jay Associates

Library of Congress Cataloging-in-Publishing Data
John Austin Murphy

Murphy Was A Lawyer...And A Quahogger: illustrated collection of observations / John Austin Murphy---1st ed.

ISBN 0-9773969-0-8

Manufactured in the United States of America

Published September, 2005

Note on Attribution of Sources

Over the years the Murphy's Law column has relied heavily on quoted materials, and the same is true of this book. Effort has been taken to accurately attribute to the proper source this quoted material. Where the source is Murphy, the lawyerin' quahogger, the particular item is followed by

Of course, has come to understand that all knowledge is derivative, and that many thinkers, even the most highly respected, may delusionally believe that a particular idea or statement originated with them. This is most certainly true in the case of

John Austin Murphy
Jamestown, Rhode Island
September, 2005

Contents

Dedication   - i -

Foreward   - ii -

Chapter One   Lawyers & the Law   1

Chapter Two   Politics and Politicians   17

Chapter Three   Religion   37

Chapter Four   Movies, Music, Sports, etc.   45

Dedication

To my father, Neale D. Murphy, whose love of humor was a
notable character trait; and, to my mother, Mary Behan, for
whom reading and learning were imperatives throughout her life.

Forward

The task of preparing on a once-a-week basis the Murphy's Law columns appearing in *The Jamestown Press* has been a source of significant personal gratification over the past ten years. Although occasionally a burden, publishing a weekly column has permitted me to "vent" on a wide variety of topics, and bring attention to those principles which I consider relevant to issues confronting our community, both local and beyond.

In carrying out this task, I have been fortunate to have had the encouragement and assistance of many people. At *The Jamestown Press*, publisher Jeff McDonough, editor Chris Irby, columnist Jim ("Walrus") Munro, and, most of all, manager Alice Dunn, have all been most supportive. In my own office, Sonya Morton-Ranney has been faithfully attentive to making sure that our copy is provided to *The Jamestown Press* in a timely fashion, and as typographically error-free as humanly possible.

I am also grateful to the many people, family and friends, who have suggested items for the column, and offered constructive commentary when it was much needed. This group includes my wife Mary Jane, my daughters, Emily and Leah, my sister Joan, and many friends and neighbors, too numerous to list here.

In putting together this book, I was indeed fortunate to have the guidance of Don Bousquet, who has successfully published many books of his cartoons. His creativity, artistic skill, and sense of humor speak for themselves in the pages that follow. But I was also the beneficiary of his generous sharing of knowledge, without which this book would not exist.

Also of great importance to the creation of this book was the invaluable help of my editor, Liz Abbott, and my graphic designer, Spencer Berger. It was Liz Abbott who taught me the hard lesson of paring down the text to a tight, concise, and readable collection. "Killing your children," as Liz so aptly put it. Leaving out certain favorite items has been an absolutely wrenching experience for me. But I am happy that Liz did her job well, as harsh as that job may occasionally be. Designer Spencer Berger made it all look good, and put the textual copy and illustrations in what seems to us to be the best possible format.

Of course, the Murphy's Law column and this book would not exist without the expressions of wisdom and wit from the great minds quoted throughout each.

John Austin Murphy
Jamestown, Rhode Island
September, 2005

Chapter One

LAWYERS & THE LAW

"I like no law at all; Were there no law, there'd be no law-breakers.
So all men would be virtuous."

— *Oscar Wilde (1854-1900)*

"I, myself, have never worked hard. I spent my time playing
cards when I was an undergraduate at Brown University."

— *Supreme Court Chief Justice Charles Evan Hughes (1862-1948)*

LAWYER: "Sir, were you shot in the fracas?"

WITNESS: "No, I was shot midway between the fracas and the navel."

"Besides the apparent foolishness inherent in asking the ignorant to use
the incomprehensible to decide the unknowable, recognition seems to be
growing that jury justice is delayed, inefficient, and tinged with unfairness."
— *Judge Hiller B. Zobel* *(1932 -)* Massachusetts Superior Court

"Lawsuit, n. A machine which you go into as a pig and come out a sausage."
— *Ambrose Bierce (1842-1914)*

"It is the trade of lawyers to question everything, yield nothing, and to talk by the hour."
— *Thomas Jefferson (1743-1826)*

"SOME CIRCUMSTANTIAL EVIDENCE IS VERY STRONG,
AS WHEN YOU FIND A TROUT IN THE MILK."

- HENRY D. THOREAU, 1817-1862

"It ain't no sin if you crack a few laws now and then, just so long as you don't break any."

— *Mae West (1893-1980)*

"Never did he cease to regard a Supreme Court appointment
as vastly more desirable than the Presidency."

— *Mrs. William Taft (1861-1943)*
Wife of William Howard Taft (1857-1930), the only president in
U.S. history to also serve as Chief Justice of the United States Supreme Court.

Lawyer (over the phone):   "They can't put you in jail for doing that."

Client: "Oh yeah? Where do you think I'm calling from - the library?"

"I COULD CARVE OUT OF A BANANA A JUDGE WITH MORE BACKBONE..."
– OLIVER WENDELL HOLMES, 1809–1894

It was a scorching hot day in Kentucky and Abe Lincoln's client had just been convicted of a felony. The judge allowed a recess, so all could take a drink outside the courthouse. Lincoln's client never returned. The prosecutor suggested that Lincoln told his client to flee, but the future President responded that, as an officer of the court, he would never do that. But, Lincoln allowed, he might have told the defendant that they had some mighty fine drinking water in Tennessee.

— *Lincoln lore*

"I will not say … that The Law will admit of no rival … but I will say that it is a jealous mistress, and requires a long and constant courtship."

— *Joseph Story (1779-1849)*

LAWYER: "Have you lived in this town your whole life?"

WITNESS: "Not yet."

LAWYER: "DOCTOR DID YOU SAY THE VICTIM WAS SHOT IN THE WOODS?"
WITNESS: "NO, I SAID HE WAS SHOT IN THE LUMBAR REGION."

"Litigant, *n.* A person about to give up his skin for the hope of retaining his bones."
— *Ambrose Bierce (1842-1914)*

In 1878, a jury awarded damages of a farthing - less than a penny - to artist James Abbott McNeill Whistler in his libel suit against art critic John Ruskin. Ruskin had called Whistler an "impudent coxcomb" for asking two hundred guineas for 'Nocturne in Black and Gold,' a painting he likened to "flinging a pot of paint in the public's face." In a show of disgust with Whistler's lawsuit, the jury also ordered the artist to pay Ruskin's legal bills.

"He that goes to law holds a wolf by the ears."
— *Robert Burton (1577-1640)*

JUDGE: "I am going to issue a warrant to have the defendant arrested."

LAWYER: "You can't do that! My client is a schizophrenic."

JUDGE: "In that case, I'll issue two warrants."

Asked why the Supreme Court commanded more respect in Washington, D.C. than any other institution, Justice Louis D. Brandeis, (1846-1941), replied, "Because we do our own work."

"It is emphatically the province and duty of the judicial department to say
what the law is ... If two laws conflict with each other, the courts must
decide on the operation of each ... This is the very essence of judicial duty."
— *Chief Justice John Marshall (1755-1835)*

"IT IS BEST THAT THE LAWS BE SO CONSTRUCTED SO AS TO LEAVE
AS LITTLE AS POSSIBLE TO THE DECISION OF THOSE WHO JUDGE."
— ARISTOTLE (382–322 BC)

JURY FOREMAN: "Your honor, we find the defendant not guilty of stealing hogs."

DEFENDANT: "Your honor, does this mean I can keep the hogs?"

"Why is there always a secret singing when a lawyer cashes in?
Why does a hearse horse snicker (when) hauling a lawyer away?"

— *Carl Sandburg* (1878-1967)

People often unwittingly give up - or overestimate - their legal
rights because of bogus or incomplete advice from non-lawyers.

QUESTION: "HOW DID YOU DO IN YOUR LAWSUIT AGAINST THE MAN WHOSE DOG BIT YOU?"

ANSWER: "HIS LAWYER PROVED I BIT THE DOG."

- FROM BERT LIPPINCOTT'S (1897-1985) "JAMESTOWN SAMPLER"

Once, says an author, where I need not say,
Two travelers found an oyster on their way.
Both fierce, both hungry, the dispute grew strong,
When scale in hand, Dame Justice passed along.
Before her each with clamor pleads the laws,
Explains the matter, and would win the cause.

Dame Justice, weighing long the doubtful right,
Takes, opens, swallows it before their sight.
The cause of strife removed so rarely well,
"There, there," says Justice, "take you each a shell,
We thrive in courthouses on fools like you.
Twas a fat oyster; live in peace - adieu."

— *Alexander Pope (1688-1744)*

On edible bivalve mollusks: For food snobs, an oyster is to a quahog as the federal court is to the small claims court. But many Rhode Islanders know better.

THE JUDICIARY'S LACK OF TAXING AUTHORITY, AND DEPENDENCE
UPON THE EXECUTIVE FOR THE ENFORCEMENT OF ORDERS, HAS
CAUSED IT TO BE REGARDED AS "THE LEAST DANGEROUS BRANCH."

Chapter Two

POLITICS & POLITICIANS

"Everything is changing. People are taking the comedians seriously and the politicians as a joke."
— *Will Rogers (1879-1935)*

POLLSTER: "Are low voter turnouts due to ignorance or to apathy?"

CITIZEN: "I don't know and I don't care."

"Under democracy, one party always devotes its chief energies to trying to prove that the other party is unfit to rule - and both commonly succeed, and are right."
— *H.L. Mencken (1880-1956)*

WADDAYA MEAN NEPOTISM? HE'S MY BROTHER!

"WHADDAYA MEAN NEPOTISM? HE'S MY BROTHER!"

– PHILADELPHIA MAYOR FRANK RIZZO (1920–1991)

"When a man assumes a public trust, he should consider himself as a public property."

— *Thomas Jefferson (1743-1826)*

"It could probably be shown by facts and figures that there is no distinctly native American criminal class except Congress."

— *Mark Twain* from "The Tragedy of Pudd'nhead Wilson," 1894.

"The arts of power and its minions are the same in all countries and in all ages. It marks the victim; denounces it; and excites the public odium and the public hatred, to conceal its own abuses and encroachments."

— *Henry Clay (1777-1852)*

"MY AFTERNOON NAPS KEEP ME FROM MEDDLING IN AFFAIRS OF STATE."
– PRESIDENT CALVIN COOLIDGE (1872–1933)

"The greatest danger to liberty lurks in insidious encroachment
by men of zeal, well-meaning but without understanding."

— *Chief Justice Louis D. Brandeis (1856-1941)*

"That man can pack the most words into the least ideas of any man I know."

— *Abraham Lincoln (1809-1865)*

"I not only 'don't choose to run' (for President) but
I don't even want to leave a loophole in case I am drafted."

— *Will Rogers (1879-1935)*

"WHEN I DIE - IF I DIE - I WANT TO BE BURIED IN
LOUISIANA SO I CAN STAY ACTIVE IN POLITICS."
- GOVERNOR EARL K. LONG (1895-1960)

The importance of courage and determination, as demonstrated by Abraham Lincoln (1809-1865):

Life event	At age
Failed in business	22
Defeated for Legislature	23
Failed in business, again	24
Elected to Legislature	25
Sweetheart dies	26
Nervous breakdown	27
Defeated for Speaker	29
Defeated for Elector	31
Defeated for Congress	34
Elected to Congress	37
Defeated for Congress	39
Defeated for Senate	46
Defeated for Vice President	47
Defeated for Senate	49
Elected President of the United States	51

— Lincoln lore

"IF YOU WANT A FRIEND IN WASHINGTON, GET A DOG."
– HARRY TRUMAN (1884–1972)

"The liberal philosophy holds that enduring governments must be accountable to someone beside themselves; that a government responsible only to its own conscience is for long tolerable."

— *Walter Lippmann (1889-1974)*

"This is the place to get a poor opinion of every body."

— *Mark Twain (1835-1910),*
watching the impeachment trial of President Andrew Johnson.

"The American people have got so used to quacks in high office that they have come to feel uneasy in the presence of honest men."

— *H.L. Mencken (1880-1956)*

"WE HAVE A GOVERNMENT THAT MAKES
WINSTON CHURCHILL SOUND LIKE A PACIFIST CLERGYMAN."
– JON CARROLL (1957)

"When I make a mistake, it's a beaut!"

— *Fiorello LaGuardia* *(1882-1947)*

At midnight, a mounted messenger from the Capitol clip-clopped to the
White House, dismounted, and was ushered up to the President's bedside.
"Mr. President, the Congress has adjourned," he said.
The President sat up in bed. "The Republic is saved," he said.

— *The Washington Spectator*

"Democracy substitutes election by the incompetent
many for appointment by the corrupt few."

— *George Bernard Shaw* *(1856-1950)*

— SENIOR U.S. SENATOR STROM THURMOND (1902-2003)

AS QUOTED BY HUMORIST DAVE BARRY.
TRANSLATION: "SOMEONE HAS COLORED MY HAIR
WITH WHAT APPEARS TO BE TANG BREAKFAST DRINK."

"If I'm alive, what am I doing here? And if I'm dead, why do I have to go to the bathroom?"

— *Thomas Dewey (1902-1971)*
in 1948, when he awoke to discover that he lost the presidential election to Harry Truman (1884-1972).

"Politics has got so expensive that it takes a lot of money to even get beat with."

— *Will Rogers (1879-1935)*

"He never said a word of importance in the Senate and he never did a thing. But somehow with his books and his Pulitzer Prizes he managed to create the image of himself as a shining intellectual, a youthful leader who would change the face of the country. Now, I will admit that he had a good sense of humor and he looked awfully good on the goddamn television screen and through it all he was a pretty decent fellow, but his growing hold on the American people was simply a mystery to me."

— *L.B.J. (1908-1973)*
describing J.F.K. (1917-1963)

WHEN I SAY, B.S. I DON'T MEAN "BONNET SHORES"!

– BESS TRUMAN

UPON BEING ADVISED THAT HER HUSBAND SHOULD USE THE WORD "FERTILIZER" RATHER THAN "MANURE." "YOU DON'T UNDERSTAND. IT'S TAKEN ME TWENTY YEARS TO GET HIM TO SAY 'MANURE'."

"People do not vote for presidential candidates in this country; they vote against them. Thus, the election is usually the butchery of a villain rather than the exaltation of a hero."

— *H.L. Mencken (1880-1956)*

"These unhappy times call for ... plans... that put their faith once more in the forgotten man at the bottom of the pyramid."

— *Franklin Delano Roosevelt (1882-1945)*

"He'd come in just like a tidal wave sweeping all over the place. He went through walls. He'd come through a door, and he'd take a whole room over. Just like that ... He was not delicate ... he was not a ballet dancer. He was a downfield blocker and a running fullback all at the same time."

— *Hubert Humphrey (1911-1978)*
describing L.B.J.

"CAPITAL PUNISHMENT IS OUR SOCIETY'S RECOGNITION OF THE SANCTITY OF HUMAN LIFE."

– U.S. SENATOR ORRIN HATCH (1934 –)

"We must remember not to judge any public servant by any one act, and especially should be aware of attacking the men who are merely the occasions and not the causes of disaster."

— *Theodore Roosevelt (1858-1919)*

"I know of no safe depository of the ultimate powers of the society but the people themselves; and if we think them not enlightened enough to exercise their control with a wholesome discretion, the remedy is not to take it from them, but to inform their discretion."

— *Thomas Jefferson (1743-1826)*

"More men have been elected between sundown and sunup than ever were elected between sunup and sundown."

— *Will Rogers (1879-1935)*

WHICH LEADER WAS A DECORATED WAR HERO, A VEGETARIAN,
NON-SMOKER, A DRINKER OF ONLY AN OCCASIONAL BEER,
AND NEVER HAD ANY ILLICIT AFFAIRS?

"...first in war, first in peace, and first in the hearts of his countrymen."
— *Henry "Light-Horse Harry" Lee (1756-1818)* eulogizing George Washington.

"But he married a widow.
— *Harry Sheely* [playing with Henry Lee's alliteration]

An elfin man, not much more than five feet tall, Senator Theodore
Francis Green (1867-1966), nevertheless, "stood up to" the towering Lyndon Johnson,
a man who, on occasion, relied upon his substantial physicality to get his way.

"NEWT"

NEWT GINGRICH, AN OUTSPOKEN SUPPORTER OF
"THREE TERMS AND YOU'RE OUT" TERM LIMITS, SERVED
EIGHT TERMS IN THE HOUSE OF REPRESENTATIVES.

Chapter Three

RELIGION

"No seed shall perish which the soul hath sown."
— *John Addington Symonds (1840-1893)*

"Indeed, I tremble for my country when I reflect that God is just."
— *Thomas Jefferson (1743-1826)*

The phrase "under God" was not in the original
Pledge of Allegiance. It was added by a joint resolution of
Congress and approved by the President on June 14, 1954.

HERBERT C. HOOVER WAS THE FIRST QUAKER TO SERVE AS
PRESIDENT OF THE UNITED STATES. THE SECOND WAS . . . ?

"The chessboard is the world; the pieces are the phenomena of the universe; the rules of the game are what we call the laws of Nature. The player on the other side is hidden from us. We know that his play is always fair, just and patient. But also we know, to our cost, that he never overlooks a mistake, or makes the smallest allowance for ignorance."

— *Thomas Henry Huxley (1825-1895)*

"The minister gave out his text and droned along monotonously through an argument that was so prosy that many a head by and by began to nod - and yet it was an argument that dealt in limitless fire and brimstone and thinned the predestined elect down to a company so small as to be hardly worth the saving."

— *Mark Twain (1835-1910)*
From "The Adventures of Tom Sawyer"

"My atheism, like that of Spinoza, is true piety towards the universe and denies only gods fashioned by men in their own image, to be servants of their human interests."

— *George Santanyana (1863-1952)*

"I circle around God, around the primordial tower. I've been circling for thousand of years and I still don't know: am I a falcon, a storm, or a great song?"

— *Rainer Maria Rilke (1875-1926)*

"God is subtle but he is not malicious."

— *Albert Einstein (1880-1952)*

– REV. PAT ROBERTSON (1930 –)

"ACTUALLY, THERE HAVE BEEN AT LEAST FIVE."

Gregorian chant: The first soul music.

And lo, Three Wise Women arrived from the East
Passing Three Kings, laden with gifts
The Women cleaned the stable
Cooked a casserole
Washed the clothes
And helped to deliver the Baby
All before the Kings arrived.

— *Anonymous*

"SAINT, n. A dead sinner revised and edited."

— *Ambrose Bierce (1842-1914)*

Chapter Four

MOVIES, MUSIC, SPORTS, etc.

"The key to acting is sincerity - once you learn to fake it, the rest is easy."
— *Sir Laurence Olivier* *(1907-1989)*

"The newspapers! Sir, they are the most villainous - licentious - abominable - infernal - not that I ever read them - no I make it a rule never to look into a newspaper."
— *Richard Brinsley Sheridan* *(1751-1816)*
from *The Critic*, Act. 1 - 1779

"Journalism largely consists of saying "Lord Jones is dead"
to people who never knew he was alive."
— *G.K. Chesterton* *(1874-1936)*

"BRACE YOURSELF, BRIDGET: THE IRISH SEX MANUAL," BY ANONONYMOUS

"Writing isn't hard. You just sit down at the typewriter, open a vein and bleed."

— *Red Smith (1905-1982)*

"Somehow I suspect that if Shakespeare were alive today,
he might be a jazz fan himself."

— *Duke Ellington (1899-1974)*

A high point in western civilization: Bobby Donaldson's drum solo on "Sing, Sing, Sing,"
performed by the Benny Goodman octet on March 26, 1955 at Basin Street.

"THE MAN WHO MISTOOK HIS WIFE FOR A HAT", BY OLIVER SACKS

"... a newspaperman ought to use his power on behalf of those getting the dirty end of the deal."
— *I.F. Stone (1907 -)*

"The Host of the Air" by William Butler Yeats: Poetry straight from the Celtic soul.

"Freedom of the press is guaranteed only to those who own one."
— *A.J. Liebling (1904-1963)*

"YOU CAN MAKE A STRADIVARIUS VIOLIN" BY JOSEPH V. REID

Great performances by child actors:
Justin Henry in *Kramer vs Kramer*
Anna Paquin in *The Piano*
Tatum O'Neal in *Paper Moon*

"Rock journalism is people who can't write,
interviewing people who can't talk, for people who can't read."

— *Frank Zappa (1940-1993)*

"Man, if you gotta ask, you'll never know."

— *Louis Armstrong (1901-1971)* when asked to define jazz.

"THIS IS MY LAND. SOME DAY I WILL BUILD ON MY LAND."

– WOODY ALLEN'S "WAR & PEACE."

An example of how times have changed in professional sports:
In 1959, after a drop in his batting average, Ted Williams demanded
that his salary be LOWERED by $35,000, from $125,000 to $90,000.

"You got to have smelt a lot of mule manure before you can sing like a hillbilly."

— *Hank Williams (1923 -1953)*

"He was a skinny kid with big ears and yet what he did to women
was something awful. And he did it every night, everywhere he went."

— *Tommy Dorsey (1905-1956),* describing the young Frank Sinatra

GERTRUDE EDERLE (1906–2003)
THE FIRST WOMAN TO SWIM THE ENGLISH CHANNEL.
SHE BEAT THE MEN'S RECORD BY HOURS.

"He was one of the wisest and most likeable ...he was clown and oracle, wit and scoundrel. Like Shakespeare (1564-1616), he had an understanding of all people and all their feelings. He was an eloquent spokesman for the human soul which dwells in us all."

— *Les Blank* (1935 -), talking about Texas bluesman Sam "Lightnin" Hopkins (1912 -)

Ray Charles' greatest live performance: Newport Jazz Festival, 1958.

"And the lion shall lie down with the lamb; but the lamb is not going to get much sleep."

— *Woody Allen (1935 -)*

"A LITTLE PIGEON TOAD" BY FRED GWYNNE

Chapter Five

MISCELLANEOUS

"Happiness is having a large, loving, caring close-knit family in another city."
— George Burns (1896-1996)

"The thing that impresses me most about Americans is the way parents obey their children."
— The Duke of Windsor, Edward VIII (1894-1972)

"No one appreciates the very special genius of your conversation as a dog does."
— Christopher Morley (1890-1957)

"FISHING IS THE OLDEST NORTH AMERICAN INDUSTRY,
BEGINNING NEARLY 400 YEARS AGO."

"People who snore always fall asleep first."

— *Anonymous*

"To cease smoking is the easiest thing I ever did.
I ought to know because I've done it a thousand times."

— *Mark Twain (1835-1910)*

"Between two evils, I always pick the one I never tried before."

— *Mae West (1892-1980)*

HE WHO GOES FORTH WITH A FIFTH ON THE FOURTH
MAY NOT COME FORTH ON THE FIFTH.

"Is that a gun in your pocket, or are you just glad to see me?"

— *Mae West (1892-1980)*

"I never put off until tomorrow what I can possibly do - the day after."

— *Oscar Wilde (1854-1900)*

"I am no good at anything but painting and gardening."

— *Claude Monet (1840-1926)*

WASH A PIG AS MUCH AS YOU LIKE,
IT GOES RIGHT BACK TO THE MUD.

"He who is without sin ... better pick some up!"

"The difference between genius and stupidity is that genius has its limits."
— *Albert Einstein* (1879-1955)

"A liar needs a good memory."
— *Quintilian* (35-95 AD)

IF YOU CHASE TWO RABBITS, BOTH WILL GET AWAY.

"Progress was all right. Only it went on too long."[1]
— *James Thurber (1894-1961)*

"If A is a success in life, then A equals X plus Y plus Z.
Work is X; Y is play; and Z is keeping your mouth shut."
— *Albert Einstein (1879-1955)*

"Blessed is he who expects nothing, for he shall never be disappointed. "
— *Jonathan Swift (1667-1745)*

WHEN WRESTLING A GORILLA ...
"YOU DON'T QUIT WHEN YOU'RE TIRED –
YOU QUIT WHEN THE GORILLA IS TIRED."

– ROBERT STRAUSS (1918 –), U.S. DIPLOMAT

"In Italy, for 30 years under the Borgias, they had warfare, terror, murder and bloodshed but they produced Michaelangelo, Leonardo da Vinci and the Renaissance. In Switzerland, they had brotherly love, 500 years of democracy and peace and what did they produce? The cuckoo clock!"

— *Orson Welles (1915-1985)*

"If you don't know where you are going, you'll almost certainly end up somewhere else."

— *Yogi Berra (1925 -)*

"There's no good answer to a stupid question."

IF YOU LOOK LIKE YOUR PASSPORT PHOTO,
YOU'RE TOO SICK TO TRAVEL.

"Take some more tea," the March Hare said to Alice very earnestly.
"I've had nothing yet. So I can't take more," Alice replied in an offended tone.
"You mean you can't take less," said the Hatter. "It's very easy to take more than nothing."

— Alice's Adventures in Wonderland
Lewis Carroll (1832-1898)

"He was a beer drinker who thought wine was for
Frenchmen or effete social climbers like his children."

— Pat Conroy (1945 -), speaking of his father, Col. Don Conroy, USMC.

"Trust your instincts. Your mistakes might as well be your own instead of someone else's."

— Billy Wilder, (1906-2002)

"CHARACTER IS DOING WHAT'S RIGHT WHEN NO ONE'S LOOKING."
- CONGRESSMAN J.C. WATTS (1957 -)

"Don't look back. Something might be gaining on you."
— *Satchel Paige (1906-1982)*

"Character is like a tree and reputation like its shadow.
The shadow is what we think of; the tree is the real thing."
— *Abraham Lincoln (1809-1865)*

"There is only one thing in the world worse than
being talked about, and that is not being talked about."
— *Oscar Wilde (1854-1900)*

"...BEING IN A SHIP IS BEING IN A JAIL WITH THE CHANCE
OF BEING DROWNED...A MAN IN A JAIL HAS MORE ROOM,
BETTER FOOD, AND COMMONLY BETTER COMPANY."
— SAMUEL JOHNSON (1696-1772)

Around the Corner

Around the corner I have a friend
In this great city that has no end;
Yet days go by, and weeks rush on,
And before I know it a year is gone,
And I never see my old friend's face,
For Life is a swift and terrible race.

He knows I like him just as well
As in the days when I rang his bell
And he rang mine. We were younger then,
And now we are busy, tired men;
Tired with playing a foolish game,
Tired with trying to make a name.

"Tomorrow," I say, "I will call on Jim,
Just to show that I'm thinking of him."
But tomorrow comes - and tomorrow goes,
And the distance between us grows and grows
Around the corner! - yet miles away ..."
Here's a telegram, sir ...
Jim died today
And that's what we get and deserve in the end
Around the corner, a vanished friend.

— *Charles Hanson Towne (1877-1949)*

"WHEN DID WE GET SO [EXPLETIVE] THIRSTY?"
- GEORGE CARLIN (1937 -)

"A meaningful apology should not contain the words "if" or "but.""

"The Irish are a fair people; they never speak well of one another."
— *Samuel Johnson* (1696-1772)

"I'm not old, but I've been used hard and put away wet."
— *Andy Dygert* Colorado hunting guide, as told to

THE DEFINITION OF **PANDERING** SHOULD CONTAIN
A DRAWING OF A LICENSE PLATE WITH AN **FOP** INSIGNIA.

"Civilization exists by geologic consent, subject to change without notice."

— *Will Durant (1885-1981)*

"Who has deceived thee so often as thyself?"

— *Benjamin Franklin (1706-1790)*

"Once I Wasn't.
Then I Was.
Now I ain't again."

— *found on a Mississippi gravestone.*

"It is best that the laws be so constructed as to leave as
little as possible to the decision of those who judge."
— *Aristotle (382-322 BC)*

"If the Lord had intended things to be bigger,
he would have made man bigger — in brains and character."
— *Louis Brandeis (1856-1941)*

"Some yuppies here wouldn't know 'rural character' if it bit them on the buns.
They think that farms smell like flowers, and lobsters are born red.""